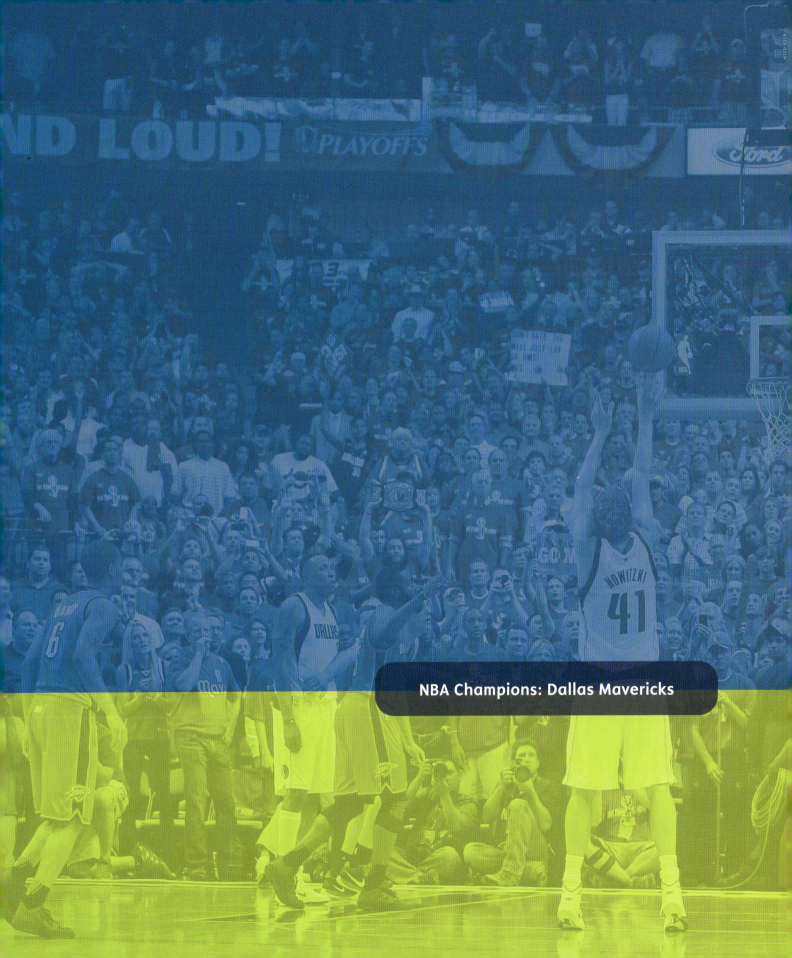
NBA Champions: Dallas Mavericks

Point guard Steve Nash

NBA CHAMPIONS

DALLAS MAVERICKS

JOE TISCHLER

CREATIVE EDUCATION / CREATIVE PAPERBACKS

Power forward Shawn Marion

Published by Creative Education and Creative Paperbacks
P.O. Box 227, Mankato, Minnesota 56002
Creative Education and Creative Paperbacks are imprints of
The Creative Company
www.thecreativecompany.us

Art Direction by Tom Morgan
Book production by Graham Morgan
Edited by Grace Cain

Images by Getty Images/Andy Lyons, 12, Bill Baptist, 5, Fernando Medina, 4, Fort Worth Star-Telegram, 1, Glenn James, 2, Joe Robbins, 3, John Biever, 16, Kevork Djansezian, cover, 7, Sam Hodde, cover, 10, Tim Heitman, 20, Stephen Dunn, 6, 15, Westend61, 9; John F. Rhodes/Dallas Morning News, 19; Newscom/Jose Luis Villegas, 24
Every effort has been made to contact copyright holders for material reproduced in this book. Any omissions will be rectified in subsequent printings if notice is given to the publisher.

Copyright © 2025 Creative Education, Creative Paperbacks
International copyright reserved in all countries. No part of this book may be reproduced in any form without written permission from the publisher.

Names: Tischler, Joe, author.
Title: Dallas Mavericks / Joe Tischler.
Description: Mankato, Minnesota : Creative Education and Creative Paperbacks, 2025. | Series: Creative sports: NBA champions | Includes index. | Audience: Ages 7-10 | Audience: Grades 2-3 | Summary: "Elementary-level text and dynamic sports photos highlight the NBA championship win of the Dallas Mavericks, plus sensational players associated with the professional basketball team such as Luka Dončić"— Provided by publisher.
Identifiers: LCCN 2024014022 (print) | LCCN 2024014023 (ebook) | ISBN 9798889892533 (library binding) | ISBN 9781682776193 (paperback) | ISBN 9798889893646 (ebook)
Subjects: LCSH: Dallas Mavericks (Basketball team)—History—Juvenile literature. | Basketball players—United States—Juvenile literature.
Classification: LCC GV885.52.D34 T57 2025 (print) | LCC GV885.52.D34 (ebook) | DDC 796.323/64—dc23/eng/20240405
LC record available at https://lccn.loc.gov/2024014022
LC ebook record available at https://lccn.loc.gov/2024014023

Printed in China

Power forward Tim Thomas

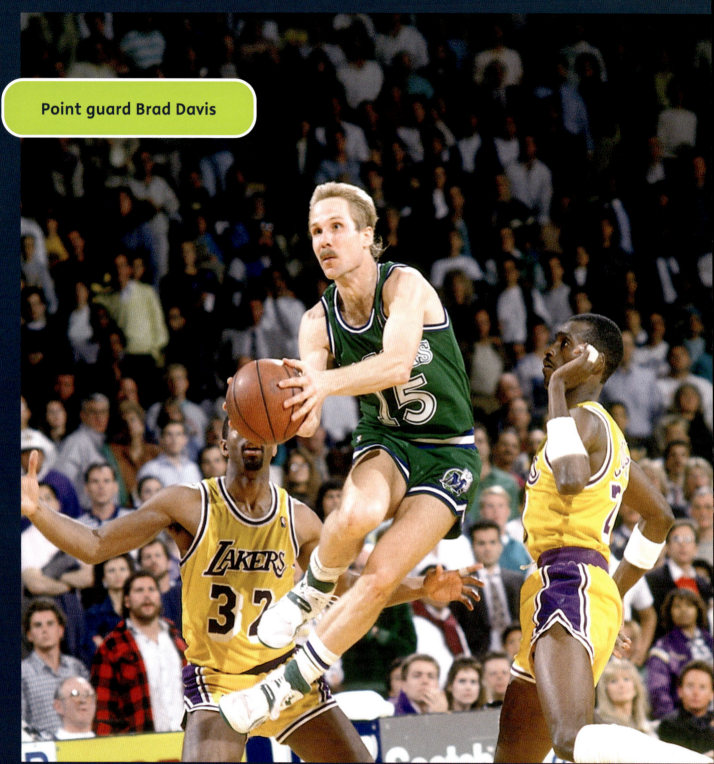
Point guard Brad Davis

CONTENTS

Home of the Mavericks	8
Naming the Mavericks	13
Mavericks History	14
Other Mavericks Stars	18
About the Mavericks	22
Glossary	23
Index	24

Home of the Mavericks

Dallas, Texas is a city well known for its cowboys. Some wear cowboy hats. Some wear football helmets. Dallas is also home to an **arena** called the American Airlines Center. It's home to a basketball team called the Mavericks.

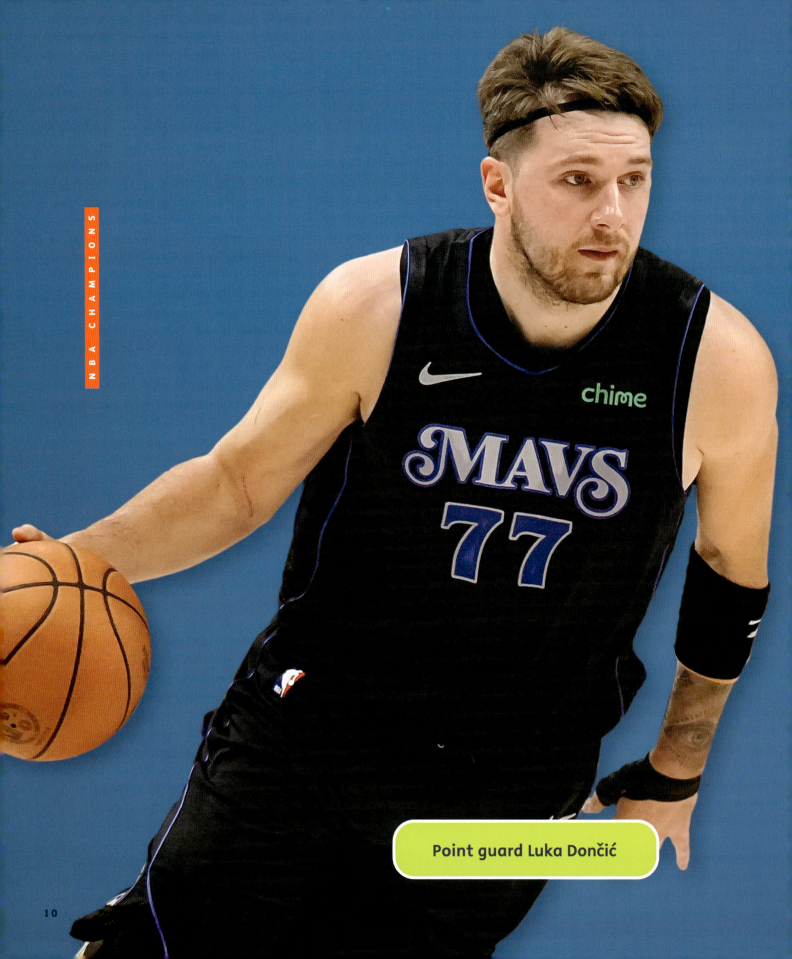

NBA CHAMPIONS

Point guard Luka Dončić

The Dallas Mavericks are a National Basketball Association (NBA) team. They play in the Southwest Division. That's part of the Western Conference. Their **rivals** are the San Antonio Spurs and Houston Rockets. All NBA teams want to win the **NBA Finals** and become champions.

NBA CHAMPIONS

Center Dwight Powell

Naming the Mavericks

The team conducted a name-the-team contest. Wranglers, Express, and Mavericks were the finalists. The team owner picked Mavericks. The nickname "represents the independent, flamboyant style of the Dallas people."

Mavericks History

The Mavericks began play in 1980. They won only 15 games their first season. They would improve. By 1984, they had 43 wins. This marked their first playoff appearance. Rolando Blackman and Mark Aguirre were early stars.

Point guard Derek Harper dished out **assists**. He played great defense, too. He led Dallas to the conference finals in 1988.

Hard times soon followed. The Mavericks missed the playoffs 10 straight seasons. In 1992–93, they

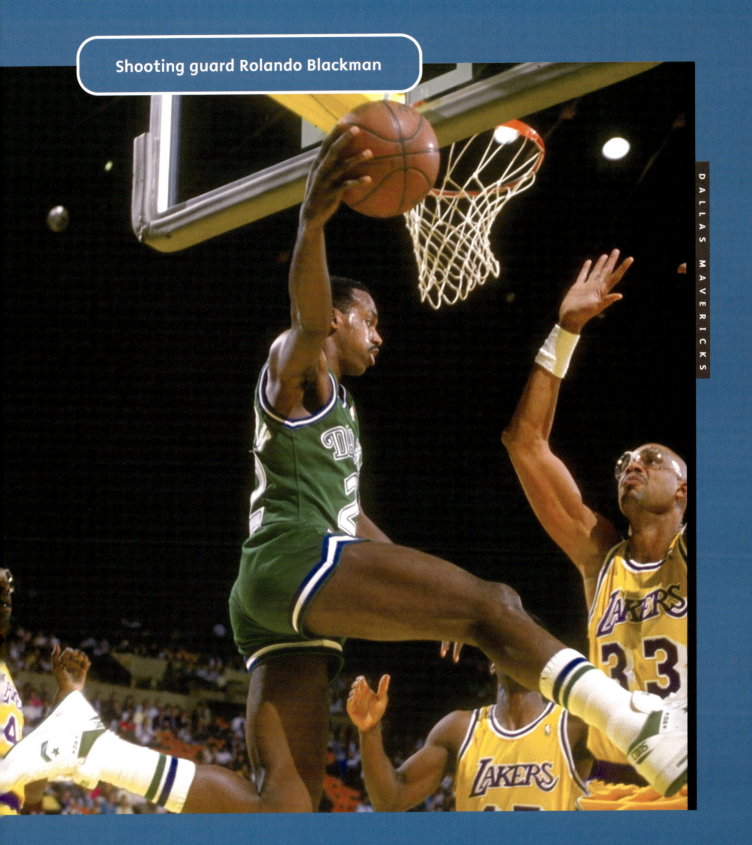

Shooting guard Rolando Blackman

NBA CHAMPIONS

Power forward Dirk Nowitzki

won only 11 games. They won just 13 games the following season. Dirk Nowitzki joined Dallas in 1998. His scoring ability helped the Mavericks win a lot more games.

Dallas reached the NBA Finals for the first time in 2006. They lost to the Miami Heat. Nowitzki was named NBA **Most Valuable Player (MVP)** the following season. Dallas won 67 games! But they lost in the first round of the playoffs. Dallas returned to the Finals in 2011. Again, they played the Heat. This time, they won! It was their first NBA **title**.

Other Mavericks Stars

Point guard Brad Davis was on the first Mavericks team. He played on the team for 12 years. Forward Sam Perkins grabbed a lot of rebounds.

Dallas picked Jason Kidd with the second pick in the 1994 NBA Draft. He was named NBA Rookie of the Year. He is now in the Hall of Fame. And

Point guard Jason Kidd

> Shooting guard Kyrie Irving

NBA CHAMPIONS

he's the team's current head coach. Steve Nash was another great point guard. He scored a lot of points. He made a lot of assists.

Today, Luka Dončić is one of the game's greatest stars. He averages more than 30 points a game. Kyrie Irving is also a great scorer. They helped Dallas reach the NBA Finals in 2024. Mavericks fans hope they can help bring another championship to Dallas soon!

About the Mavericks

First season: 1980–81

Conference/division: Western Conference, Southwest Division

Team colors: blue and silver

Home arena: American Airlines Center

NBA CHAMPIONSHIPS:

2011, 4 games to 2 over Miami Heat

TEAM WEBSITE:

https://www.mavs.com

Glossary

arena—a large building with seats for spectators, where sports games and entertainment events are held

assist—a basketball pass that leads to a basket

Most Valuable Player (MVP)—an honor given to the season's best player

NBA Finals—a series of games between two teams at the end of the playoffs; the first team to win four games is the champion

rival—a team that plays extra hard against another team

title—another word for championship

NBA CHAMPIONS

Center Shawn Bradley

Index

Aguirre, Mark, 14

American Airlines Center, 8, 22

Blackman, Rolando, 14, 15

Bradley, Shawn, 24

Davis, Brad, 6, 18

Dončić, Luka, 10, 21

Harper, Derek, 14

Irving, Kyrie, 20, 21

Kidd, Jason, 18, 19

Marion, Shawn, 4

Nash, Steve, 2, 21

Nowitzki, Dirk, 16, 17

Powell, Dwight, 12

Perkins, Sam, 18

team name, 13

Thomas, Tim, 5